D0422549

WINE

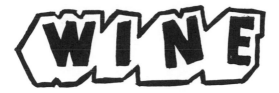

WINE

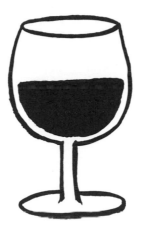

MAKES MOMMY CLEVER

CHRONICLE BOOKS

SAN FRANCISCO

First published in the United States in 2013 by Chronicle Books.

First Published in the United Kingdom in 2011 by Hodder & Stoughton,
an Hachette UK company.

Text and illustrations copyright
© 2013 by Andy Riley.

Library of Congress Cataloging-in-Publication Data

Riley, Andy.
  Wine makes mommy clever / Andy Riley.
    p. cm.
  ISBN 978-1-4521-1226-8
 1. English wit and humor, Pictorial. 2. Mothers--Caricatures and
cartoons. 3. Motherhood--Caricatures and cartoons. I. Title.

  NC1479.R55A4 2013
  741.5'6941--dc23

                              2012026423

Manufactured in China.

10 9 8 7 6 5 4 3 2 1

Chronicle Books, LLC
680 Second Street
San Francisco, California 94107
www.chroniclebooks.com

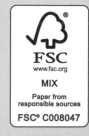

ANDY RILEY IS THE AUTHOR/ARTIST OF THE BOOK OF BUNNY SUICIDES, DAWN OF THE BUNNY SUICIDES AND EVERY OTHER BUNNY SUICIDE THING. HIS OTHER BOOKS INCLUDE GREAT LIES TO TELL SMALL KIDS, LOADS MORE LIES TO TELL SMALL KIDS, SELFISH PIGS, ROASTED AND D.I.Y. DENTISTRY.

HIS SCRIPTWRITING WORK INCLUDES BLACK BOOKS, THE GREAT OUTDOORS, HYPERDRIVE, LITTLE BRITAIN, ARMSTRONG AND MILLER, GNOMEO & JULIET, THE ARMANDO IANNUCCI SHOWS, HARRY + PAUL, SLACKER CATS AND THE BAFTA-WINNING ANIMATION ROBBIE THE REINDEER.

misterandyriley.com

WITH THANKS TO:
GORDON WISE, LISA HIGHTON,
POLLY FABER AND KEVIN CECIL.

OTHER PEOPLE'S BABIES

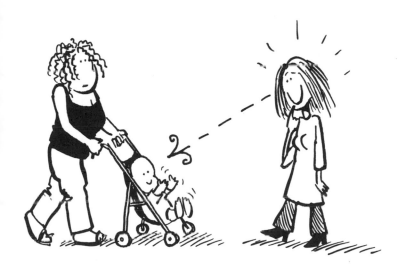

MAKE MOMMY WANT
ANOTHER ONE

OTHER PEOPLE'S TODDLERS

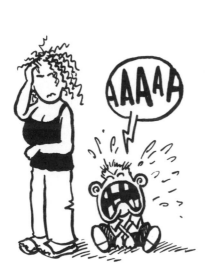
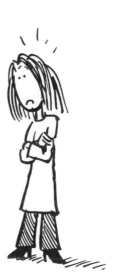

MAKE MOMMY NOT
WANT ANOTHER ONE

MOM'S LAW OF
LIPSTICK:

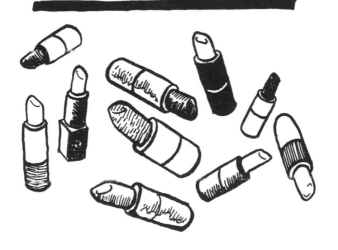

WHOEVER DIES
WITH THE MOST
COLORS **WINS**

THAT VERY FIRST PREGNANCY

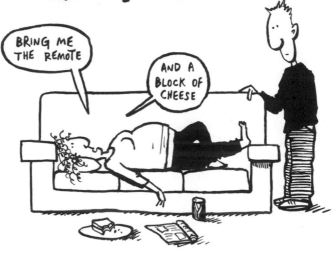

...., ALSO THE VERY LAST TIME MOMMY WILL HAVE SOMEONE ELSE DOING ALL THE FETCHING AND CARRYING

OUCH

MOMMY SUFFERS
TO LOOK SO
beautiful

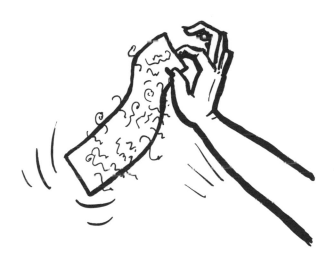

DAD'S WORST T-SHIRT

MOMMY NEVER TOLD HIM SHE THREW IT AWAY

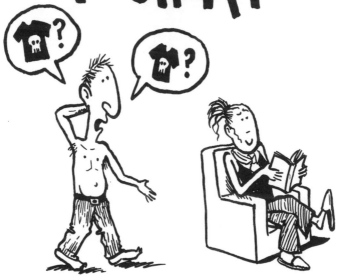

CHOCOLATE CAKE

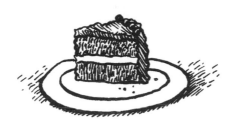

MOMMY KNOWS
IT'S WRONG

BUT IT FEELS
SO RIGHT

WEBSITES ABOUT MOTHERING

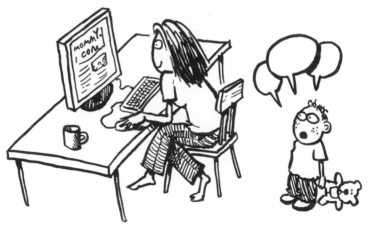

GIVE MOM TIPS TO BE A BETTER PARENT

AND HELP HER IGNORE THE KIDS
FOR TWENTY MINUTES

ALL AT THE SAME TIME

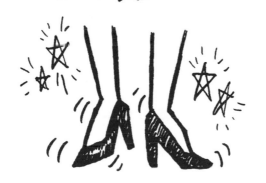

"I WILL SURVIVE"

MOMMY CAN'T NOT DANCE TO IT

MOMMY'S POTTED PLANTS

UMM... YES DARLING
OF COURSE I'VE BEEN WATERING THEM WHILE YOU'RE AWAY

...UH-OH

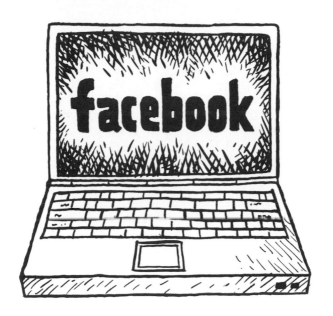

MAKES MOMMY'S
MORNING
MAGICALLY
VANISH

THE SMELL OF SUNBLOCK

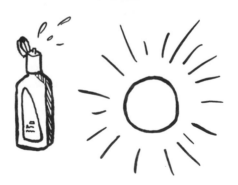

MAKES MOMMY
FEEL LIKE SHE'S ON
VACATION ALREADY

CRITICIZING DADDY

IT'S JUST MOMMY'S WAY OF IMPROVING HIM

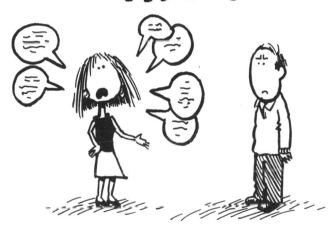

MUFFINS

MOMMY'S "EARNED ONE"
'ROUND ABOUT 4 PM
EVERY DAY

MOM'S ROMANTIC TRIP AWAY

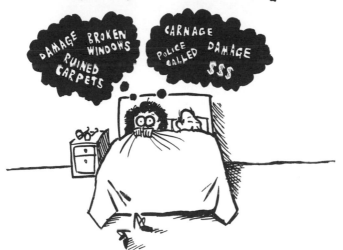

— SPENT IN CONSTANT FEAR
THAT HER TEENAGERS
ARE GOING TO THROW
A HOUSE PARTY

MOMMY'S FINGER

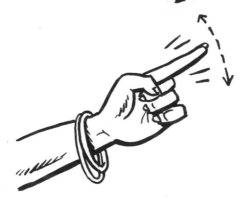

DON'T MAKE IT WAG

TOO LATE!
IT'S WAGGING

EX-BOYFRIENDS

HI
SO ERRR... HOW'S IT GOING
THESE DAYS

MAKE MOMMY
FEEL AWKWARD

YET SOMEHOW
STILL ADMIRED

KILLER HEELS

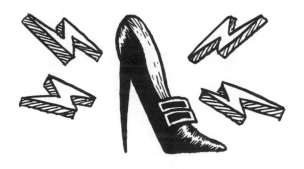

NO, MOMMY'S
NOT TOO OLD
TO WEAR THEM

KILLED

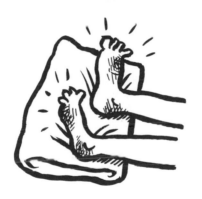

(MOMMY THE DAY
AFTER THE
KILLER HEELS)

CHILDBIRTH

HA!
HA!
HA
HA!
YOU THINK THAT HURTS

MEANS MOMMY NEVER HAS TO LISTEN TO A MAN COMPLAINING ABOUT PAIN EVER AGAIN

FASHION MISTAKES

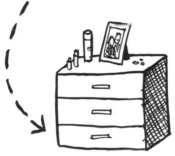

MOMMY KEEPS
THEM IN THE
BOTTOM DRAWER
OF SHAME

THE WEDDING DRESS

YES, MOMMY COULD
STILL FIT INTO IT

SHE'S JUST NOT GOING
TO TRY IT TODAY, IS ALL

CUTE INTERNET PICTURES OF CATS STICKING THEIR HEADS OUT OF SAUCEPANS

AWWW

MOMMY CAN NEVER SEE ENOUGH OF THEM

RICE
CAKES

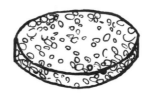

ONE DAY MOMMY WILL
CONVINCE HER STOMACH
THAT THEY MAKE A
SATISFYING MEAL

AND THEN EVERYTHING
WILL BE FINE

THE
BATH

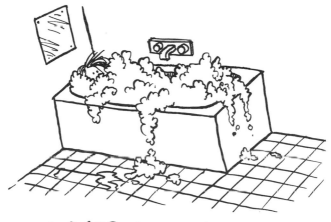

MAKES MOMMY
≥ DISAPPEAR ≥
FOR UP TO AN HOUR

DAYTIME TV

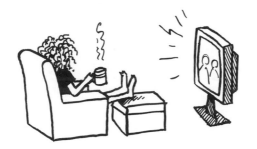

MOM TRIES TO
RATION HERSELF

NO MORE THAN
NINE HOURS A DAY

FLOWERS

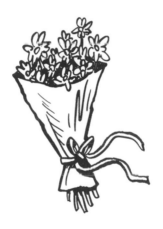

IF THEY WERE CHEAP

MOMMY CAN *ALWAYS TELL*

CLEANING

NO-ONE NOTICES IT HAPPENS

UNTIL MOMMY GOES AWAY FOR TWO DAYS

ONLINE SHOPPING

HOLY
S[redacted]

MAKES MOMMY HAPPY
(EXCEPT FOR 1 DAY A MONTH)

VACATION

IN
OUT

MOMMY NEEDS ONE

NOW

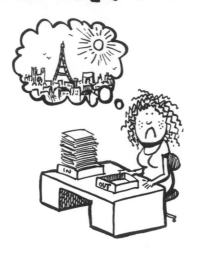

MORE
CHOCOLATE CAKE

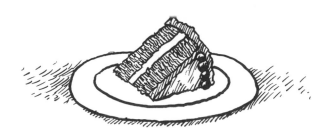

"THE SOONER IT'S ALL GONE,
THE SOONER IT'S NOT THERE
TO TEMPT ME"

THAT'S MOMMY'S REASONING

MOMMY
SPIT

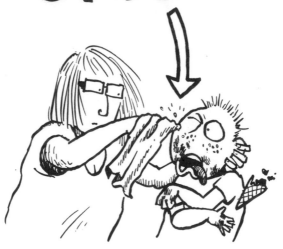

REMOVES ALL
KNOWN STAINS

THE GYM

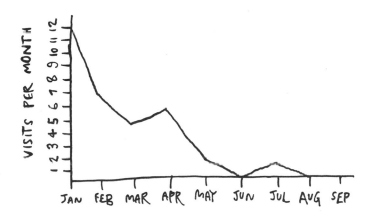

MOMMY'S STILL
A MEMBER

THE 5 SIGNS OF PROBLEM HAIR

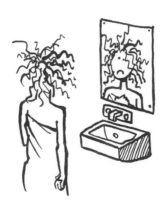

MOMMY THINKS
SHE'S GOT 7 OR
8 OF THEM

DIRTY DANCING

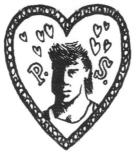

MOMMY'S SEEN IT _ _ _ TIMES

(INSERT CORRECT NUMBER HERE)

HOROSCOPES

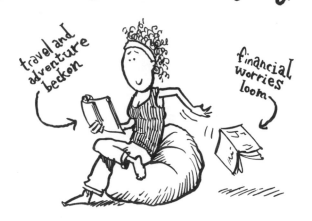

travel and adventure beckon

financial worries loom

MOMMY KNOWS TO
IGNORE THE BAD ONES

AND TRUST THE
GOOD ONES

DWTS

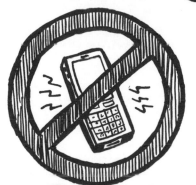

IS ON SO
DON'T
CALL MOM

LATTE
AFTER THE
SCHOOL RUN

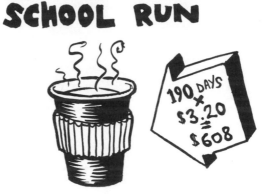

190 DAYS
+
$3.20
=
$608

RECESSION OR
NO RECESSION
MOMMY NEEDS ONE

LOUNGE CHAIR

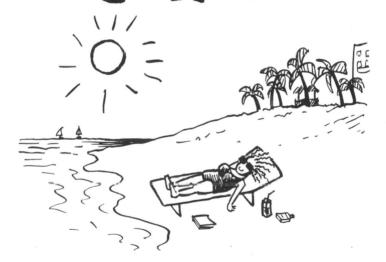

DON'T TRY TO
SHIFT MOMMY OFF IT
FOR THE NEXT 2 WEEKS

SPA
TREATMENTS

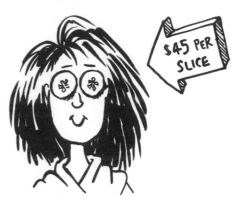

$45 PER SLICE

MOMMY LOVES THEM
ESPECIALLY WHEN
MOMMY'S NOT PAYING

YET MORE
CHOCOLATE CAKE

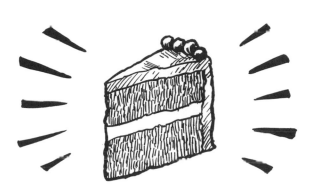

LOOK, JUST GIVE
IT TO MOMMY
NOW, OKAY?

SOCKS
IN BED

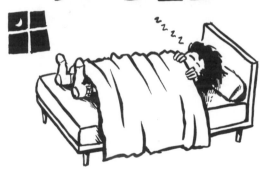

NOT VERY SEXY

BUT MOM'S GOT
TO KEEP WARM

MOM'S FANCY SHAMPOO

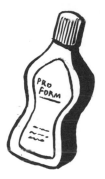

SOMEONE'S BEEN USING
IT AS *SHOWER GEL* AGAIN

SOMEONE'S GOING
TO GET *KILLED*

BOTOX

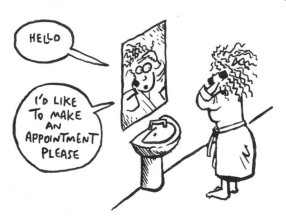

MOM'S STOPPED MAKING JOKES ABOUT CELEBRITIES WHO'VE HAD IT DONE

SOMETHING'S UP

BOOKING A BABYSITTER

WELL
THIS IS NICE
$7 PER HOUR
=11.66¢ PER MINUTE

DOESN'T PUT A BIT OF PRESSURE ON MOMMY AND DADDY TO HAVE A GOOD NIGHT OUT

DADDY'S MORNING POO

WOOF
WOULDN'T GO IN THERE FOR HALF AN HOUR IF I WAS YOU

MOMMY DOESN'T WANT TO HEAR ABOUT IT

BUT SHE GETS TO, ALL THE SAME

SHOES

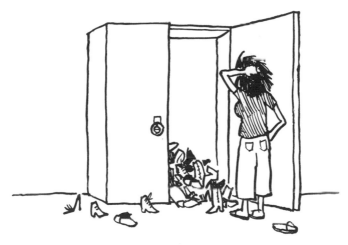

ARE SOMETHING
MOMMY WILL
DEFINITELY ORGANIZE
THIS WEEKEND,
DEFINITELY

SWIMMER'S SHOULDERS

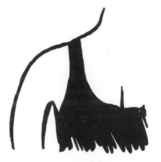

PEOPLE SOMETIMES SAY
MOMMY HAS THEM

SHE'S STILL TRYING TO
WORK OUT IF IT'S A
COMPLIMENT OR NOT

LADIES' NIGHTS

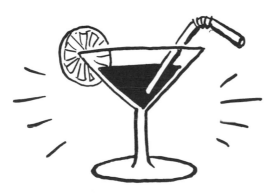

MAKE MOMMY FEEL
EIGHTEEN

THE
HAIRDRYER

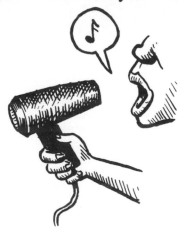

MOMMY'S MICROPHONE
(WHEN NOBODY'S LOOKING)

GRAND CHILDREN

...MOMMY'S PAYOFF
FOR ALL THAT
HARD WORK

SCENTED CANDLES

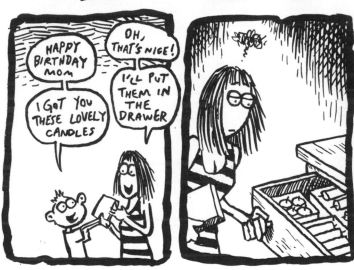

MOMMY'S GOT ENOUGH NOW, YOU CAN STOP BUYING THEM AS PRESENTS

ICE CREAM

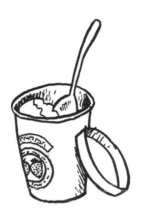

MOMMY'S DOWNFALL
(WHEN THERE'S NO
CHOCOLATE CAKE LEFT)

GROWN-UP CHILDREN

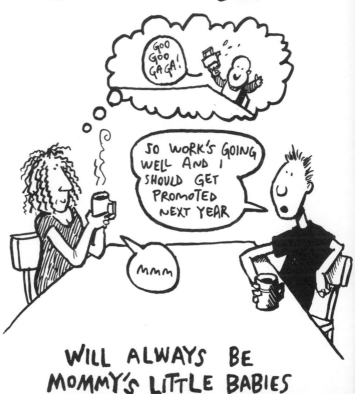

WILL ALWAYS BE
MOMMY'S LITTLE BABIES

AND

AND!!

WE LOVE MOM
THIS MUCH

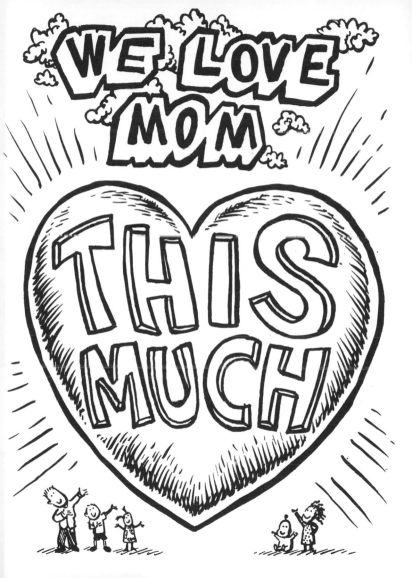

REFILL
REQUIRED